Baby's
THINGS THAT GO

Black and White
High-Contrast Book

Written and illustrated by

R. M. Smith

CLARENCE-HENRY BOOKS

Honk,
beep,
little car!

Keep it real,
work **truck!**

Hi there,
choo choo train!

Looking good,
floaty boat!

Fly up high,
airplane!

What's up,
hot air balloon?

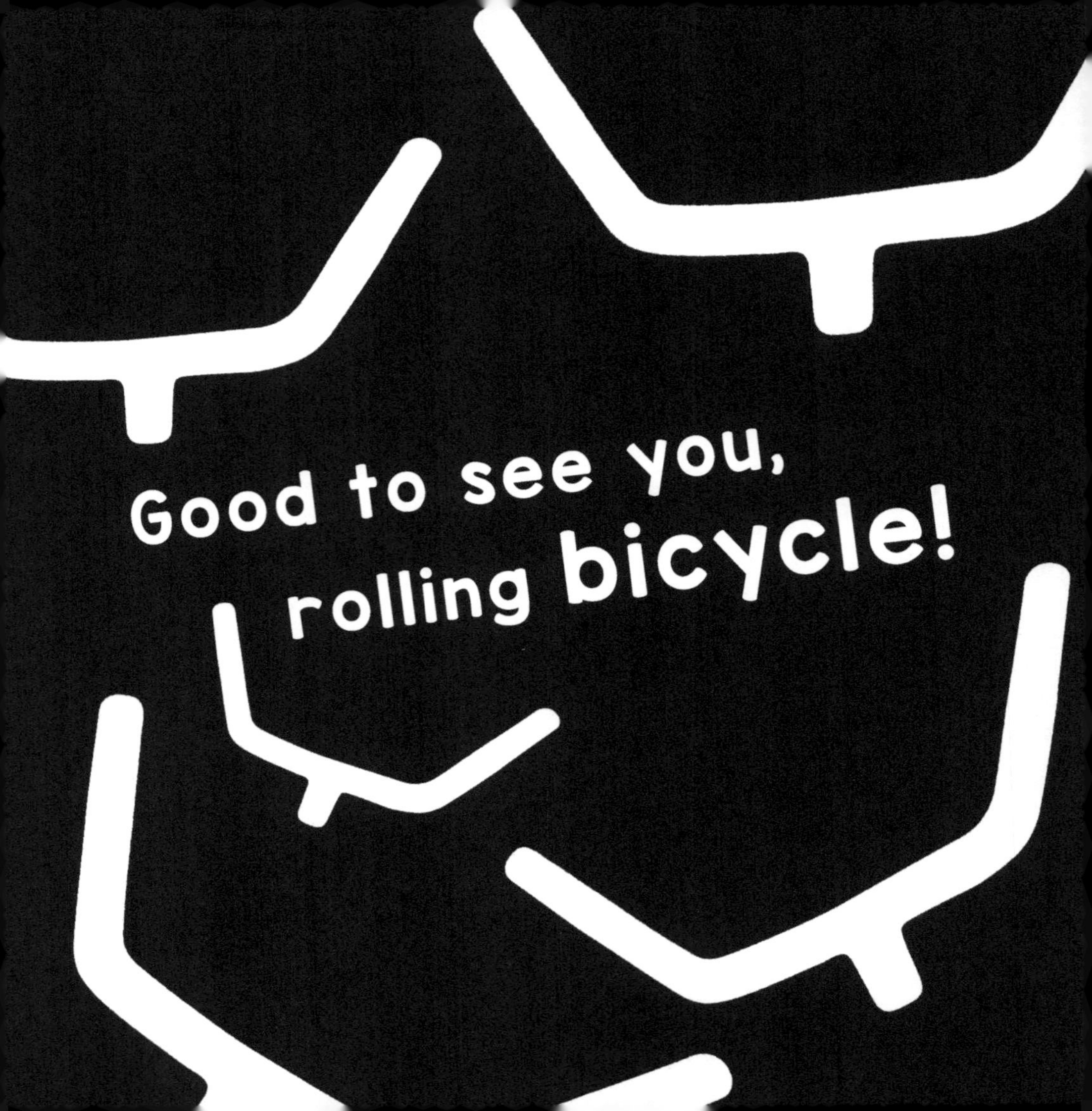
Good to see you,
rolling bicycle!

Scoot on, sleek

scooter!

Ride on,
big bus!

What's twirling,

helicopter?

Hello there,
buzzy **blimp!**

Vroom,
vroom
motorcycle!

See you later,
submarine!

Baby's
THINGS THAT GO
by R. M. Smith

Clarence-Henry Books • Alexandria, VA
Copyright © 2024 R. M. Smith

Design and Layout by R. M. Smith

Summary: A high-contrast black and white baby book
featuring things that go.

ISBN-10: 0988290979
ISBN-13: 978-0988290976

First Edition
10 9 8 7 6 5 4 3 2 1

www.ingramcontent.com/pod-product-compliance
Lightning Source LLC
Chambersburg PA
CBHW051254020426
42333CB00025B/3213